The Power And Blessings Of A Sunrise

By Barry Rice

Bountiful Tomorrows Start Here When You Accept The Tremendous Blessings & Opportunities That God Places Before You Each and Every Day

www.seeyoursunrise.com

Copyright © 2007

Published by:
Barry W. Rice
barry@seeyoursunrise.com

Dedication

Thank you, Ann, for being my rock,
my best friend and the love of my life.

INTRODUCTION

Do you believe that "living" is a life of going to work, paying your bills, raising your children, and then retiring? Or have you stopped dreaming of what else could be in your future because you're afraid you can't achieve it?

I've got news for you. It doesn't matter who or where you are or what you're doing, today is the day that your idea of "living" can open a new chapter into what your future can and will be. This is your day to sit back and begin to see the choices that are presented to you every day upon God's sunrise of opportunities, and for you to dream of what can and will be in your future.

Will you use the day to visualize and dream? While this might seem like an easy question to answer, it is for many people quite difficult and elusive.

This is your day. It's your choice what will you do with it. The power that comes with every sunrise is yours for the taking. Will you use it?

4

Our society has seen dramatic changes since the days of the founding fathers. The personal freedom and responsibility that was cherished by the early settlers has been gradually eroded by selfish ambition, greed, and a misguided notion of entitlement. These values are not what defined success and happiness two hundred years ago, and they are certainly not part of God's plan for our lives today.

When the blinders of circumstance and materialism are removed, we begin to see with the eyes of our heart, or what I call the eyes of faith. We begin to see the unseen—the plan, the power, and the purpose that God brings into our lives. We begin to understand that the path of our lives, our success, and our happiness is not determined by Madison Avenue or Washington, D.C. but by God. Then we can begin to better understand the opportunities that He presents to us on a daily basis.

With each new sunrise comes a day filled with opportunities, choices, and blessings—each one provided by God. Our attitude, outlook, and direction are determined, first, by recognizing that God provides a daily renewal every day, and second, by how we react to this reality and our willingness and personal commitment to live with purpose and in unity with God.

Will we have setbacks? Certainly. Will there be disappointment? Absolutely. But when you view through the eyes of faith, your setbacks and disappointments will offer opportunities for growth and change through the awesome Power that produces the sunrise in the first place, that Power being God. He is right there to see you through any difficulties that will inevitably cross your path.

Welcome to The Power and Blessings of A Sunrise.

The Power and Blessings of a Sunrise

Your Tomorrows Start Here With Daily Blessings and Opportunities From God!

Chapter 1

You have likely experienced moments in your life that gave you pause to reflect on your past, present, and future. We all have, and I'd like to share one such moment of my past—a moment that presented a lingering question although I didn't get the answer until later in life.

After my senior year in high school, I worked at an Easter Seal Camp for disabled children and teenagers. The camp was responsible for looking after children and young people with special physical or mental retardation needs. It was our mission to assist these campers with their personal needs when required, such as dressing, feeding, even their personal needs and assistance using the bathroom. We also assisted them in swimming classes, arts and crafts, boating, and other recreational activities.

This experience turned out to be one of the most moving and self-discovering opportunities of my life. I didn't know until this later in life, but it was through The Power and Blessings of a Sunrise and God revealing Himself to me, that I finally found the answer to the question that was posed by Mike M., a camper. Mike had been my only camper for one of the ten-day sessions.

Although at age twenty-one Mike was no longer a child, his body was twisted like a pretzel as when in his mother's womb. Since birth he had been living in a home for the incurable.

This very special human being was unable to care for himself in any manner and was relegated to being strapped into a specially built wheelchair, relying on others' assistance for literally everything. Each counselor was normally assigned two to three campers per session, but for that particular session Mike was my only charge.

Here was a young man who had no chance for any change or improvement in his physical disability. He did, however, have a zest for living that we could all benefit by emulating.

Mike had a remarkably sharp mind, was well-read with a special device on his wheelchair to hold books, and he spoke clearly. Although devoid of what most of us consider normal physical abilities, Mike continually exhibited a positive can-do attitude, a ready smile, and a hearty laugh.

One morning while I was preparing Mike for breakfast, he asked me, "Barry, people can see my disability. What's yours?"

How was I supposed to answer that? How would you?

It was a question for which I didn't have an answer. I gave it only a moment's consideration and then went on with my daily duties. Throughout the rest of the day, I thought of the question as only pertaining to my physical being. How was I supposed to answer that? How would you?

All through high school I had played basketball and even had offers of a basketball scholarship. Plus, I was involved in baseball, summers on the lake water skiing, going to dances, and taking part in all the other activities most young men enjoyed. Nothing wrong with me physically.

It wasn't until much later, after I had discovered that there were power and daily blessings in every sunrise that I finally understood what Mike had been seeing in me . . . and asking.

Mike had seen that I was empty of spirituality and that I had not learned how to see God and His daily blessings and opportunities for a rich and full life.

It was not until later in life that I learned that my disability had been my failure to look for and catch the happiness, blessings, and opportunities provided by God upon the horizon of every sunrise. I finally learned that the only permanent disabilities for anyone are in the failure to love and live life to the fullest within the limits of our individual circumstances. I was learning to lovingly accept The Power and Blessings of a Sunrise, to be ever grateful to God, and to love life as God has planned for us.

Points To Ponder

_____

_____

_____

_____

_____

_____

_____

_____

_____

Chapter II

You will feel an aura of excitement when you discover the tremendous opportunities and choices for your future as they are presented, daily, upon the horizon of the sunrise. Some of the benefits are:

- Experiencing happiness like never before

- Having peace of mind about the direction of your future

- Renewed enthusiasm for your future

- A major boost in your self-confidence and self-esteem

- Strong family relationships

- Putting financial worries behind you

- And, MOST importantly, spiritually based peace of mind

Most people get caught up in the happenings of their day and spend it trying to please everyone around them. They also spend absurd amounts of time attempting to "keep up with the Joneses." They are so busy trying to fit in that they are not seeing the invisible side of life—what I call the spiritual life. Ignoring this invisible, or spiritual side, of life is a risky and discouraging way to live.

Let me repeat that, " . . . not-seeing the invisible, or spiritual, side of life is a risky and discouraging way to live."

And what is the invisible, or spiritual, side of life?

I believe it is God!

My own disbelief must have been glaring a "disability," because Mike could see it. Quite simply, I believed that if I couldn't see God, if I couldn't reach out and touch Him, how could I possibly believe He existed, let alone send blessings my way?

Through The Power and Blessings of a Sunrise, I will prove that God is NOT invisible. I eagerly accept the challenge to lead you to seeing God and how you, too, can open your eyes and heart to receive His daily blessings and opportunities.

Points To Ponder

_____

_____

_____

_____

_____

_____

_____

_____

_____

_____

Chapter III

One evening in 1776, Benjamin Franklin was out for a leisurely dinner with friends. Their discussion had turned to the newly signed Declaration of Independence when the town drunk, who had been overhearing their conversation, stumbled over to their table. The drunken man shouted at Franklin, "Aw, them words don't mean nothin'! Where's all the happiness that Declaration thing guarantees?"

Frustrated with the interruption, Ole Ben replied simply, "My friend, the Declaration of Independence ONLY guarantees you the right to the pursuit of happiness. You have to *catch* it yourself."

Think about this. More than two hundred years ago, when early American settlers began drawing up a Constitution to govern themselves, the pursuit of happiness referred to each and every citizen's involvement to determine their own laws of living. Having the Constitution also represented the joy each individual felt in holding their fate in their own hands. The rugged individualism of those early settlers guaranteed the freedoms and opportunities we still have access to today to achieve our own fate. Whether we take advantage of our freedoms and opportunities with a heavy dose of rugged individualism - or not - is a personal choice.

Without rugged individualism and personal choice, could you be waiting for your unplanned tomorrows to accumulate and become a long list of wasted yesterdays, and maybe even a waste of your living experience?

Think about it.

The basic truth of having the freedom to make decisions and the responsibility that you are charged with to choose your future, and to be joyful in the process, is the same today as it was in Benjamin Franklin's time. It is up to you to "catch" your happiness and direct your life's course.

Let this sink in. The basic truth is that you have the freedom to make decisions for your future and the responsibility to choose your future, thus leading you to happiness in the process. But, remember, it is still your responsibility to *catch* your opportunities and happiness yourself.

- o Aren't you happiest when you understand and express your personal truth about where you are today and where you will be going in the future?

- o Aren't you happiest when you involve yourself in the process of living a rich and full life?

- o Aren't you happiest when you know you are taking positive action steps in building your future?

Points To Ponder

_____

_____

_____

_____

_____

_____

_____

_____

_____

_____

Chapter IV

My self-appointed mission is to show you how The Power and Blessings of a Sunrise is the basic truth to discovering where you are today and how you can see and receive the tremendous blessings, opportunities, strength, and guidance that God is offering you and which allow you to pursue and catch your happiness.

Let's start by developing your vision of what your future will be and how you can overcome obstacles to live the future of your dreams. We'll take a look at supporting your vision with effective goals, as long as you are willing to do, within reason, whatever it takes to achieve your goals. You'll learn how to make the all-important personal commitment to live the life you might have only dreamed of.

I'll share with you how easy it is to enjoy a successful day even when the clouds of confusion, undesirable daily situations, or unpleasant circumstances seem to be blocking the warming rays of God's sunrise.

Now, close your eyes for a moment and remember a time in your past when you took the time to watch as the sun rose into the morning sky. Focus on how you felt, and do your best to recall what you were thinking. It's not important where you were or whether anyone was with you or not.

As you watched the sun begin its climb, was it all about the awe, spectacle, and beauty of the sun rising, or . . .

- o Were you watching while something major was happening in your personal or work life at the time?

- o Do you remember if you were at a time of confusion or fear?

- o Were you expecting something, were you hopeful, were you feeling particularly joyful about something?

We'll get back to your sunrise later. Just hang on to that memory while I share my personal discovery of The Power and Blessing of a Sunrise.

The Ben Franklin story I mentioned earlier holds a particular meaning for me because for many years, I had lived my life as a skeptic. I'm not proud of it; it's just the way I was. If I couldn't see it, touch it, or feel it, then I doubted it. Until about eighteen years ago, my general mind-set was one of skepticism and, to a certain degree, distrust of anything I could not see, touch, or feel.

Like the drunk in the Ben Franklin story, my excuse to myself was, "If I couldn't see it, how could I pursue it? And, if I couldn't pursue it, how could I 'catch' it?"

With that said, up to that point in my life, I had been successful in most everything I touched—because I could see it.

My transition from seeing and believing in what I could see, touch, or feel to how I began to accept life's real opportunities as God's daily blessings—disguised as a sunrise—is where we're heading.

Believing in what I could see probably started in my early childhood. It continued through one year in college, to then performing in a professional waterskiing show at Cypress Gardens, Fla., and then on through being wounded in Vietnam. Throughout those years, I succeeded in what I could see. I could see basketball, baseball, water skis, bullets, bombs . . . and death on the battlefield.

Transitioning from my early days of feeling *un*-accepted and *un*-loved by God, and what began my personal discovery of the power and blessings that accompany every sunrise is probably best explained in a letter I wrote just a few years ago to a combat Brother who made the supreme sacrifice in Vietnam many years ago.

Dear Herman,

What's it been now, forty-six years?

Well, my Brother, I wanted to take the time to put some words to the thoughts and memories that have poured from my heart over the years. It's been a long, bumpy—at best—road since we were last together. Now that we are finally together with God – you in Heaven, me still in the earthly world - writing to you brings peace.

I smile when I recall the day after a combat assault near the base of Nui Ba Dinh when we were being resupplied with bullets and rations. As we sat on the jungle floor, waiting to be 'logged,' you pulled out a picture of your beautiful fiancée and told me how she was always so proud to call you "Her man." After enduring your stories of how you and she adored each other, I found it only fitting to assign you a nickname - "Her man," later shortening it to "Herman."

On the days when the helicopters weren't ferrying us to a new hostile landing zone, when the bullets weren't flying, and we had the time to decompress, you also always seemed to begin speaking a foreign language. No, you weren't speaking Spanish, French, or Vietnamese—but, you may as well have been. Foreign in the sense that my eyes probably glazed over as I just didn't understand.

I tried to explain to you that I had no relationship with God and couldn't—or maybe the right word is "wouldn't"—understand your language. The "language" I understood was . . .

I spent much of my early life as an orphan in foster homes in a small East Tennessee town until my adoption and my name changed to Barry Rice. Even though I had lived with one family and then another, I had a good childhood and many friends. Maybe, early on, I didn't understand the comfort and security of a Mom's hugs, but I had no basic needs that were unmet.

Throughout my childhood, I attended Sunday school and church, if for no other reason than that's where my friends were.

In Sunday school one morning, the teacher responded to one of my friend's 'out-of-left-field' questions, "Why doesn't Barry have a real mommy and daddy?"

I remember it like it was yesterday. The teacher responded that God gives babies to married couples who give birth to their own babies.

Talk about feeling UN-loved—and in front of my friends, no less!!

My friends soon started chanting and teasing me by singing "Jesus Hates Barry This I Know," in the same cadence of "Jesus Loves Me This I Know," and then they laughed and teased me that God didn't love me the way He loved them. A couple of my friends even resorted to calling me a "bastard". You know how kids can be many times. Teasing another thinking that it will make them a 'hero' in their friend's eyes.

I don't really remember all the emotions I felt—after all, I was just a kid, but I do remember how it hurt. And, it hurt a lot!! I remember not only feeling rejected by whomever my real Mommy and Daddy were, but the teasing took hold and I felt that I had been rejected by God.

It was years later that I finally got around to researching where this came from. I wasn't a student of the Bible, but I wanted to know how the teacher could come up with something that had hurt so much. I did a search for "bastard child." I found it in:

Deuteronomy 23:2: King James:

"A bastard shall not enter into the congregation of the Lord, even unto his tenth generation shall he not enter into the congregation of the Lord."

Herman, I decided, if God was going to reject me, I'd just reject Him right back.

I recall that my exterior being became like hardened steel; yet, I felt myself withdrawing, not letting anyone in, not allowing my friends to see me cry on the inside when they would tease me with their stupid little songs.

I made basketball, baseball and water skiing my life, feeling that if I excelled on the outside, my friends would like and accept me again. Well, I did excel in sports, and they did like and accept me.

Graduating from high school with the offer of a basketball scholarship, I attended one year of college, but chose the fraternity and partying route instead of basketball. My grades were horrible, and although I was given one semester to improve, I had a choice to make, and it was not difficult. The summer after my freshman year at college, I was offered a job to be a part of the water-ski show at Cypress Gardens, Florida.

Four waterski shows every day and plenty of young ladies around who knew nothing about me being a "bastard" child. The crowds applauded my skills at barefoot water skiing, jumping, and carrying girls on my shoulders as I zoomed around the show circuit on one ski. We skied during the day, partied at night, no cares in the world.

No one was teasing me that God had rejected me. I could talk about my adoptive parents (I still was having a difficult time calling them Mom and Dad). No one knew that I thought I had been rejected by God, and I had probably even forgotten about it because I was having so much fun.

I blocked God so far out of my mind, that even hearing His name, I turned away from the conversation and looked for another opportunity to ski or another skier to talk to.

I was in an element so far away from God, or even thinking of Him . . . and just who was this Jesus Christ fellow, anyway?

After two years of skiing, playing, not having a care in the world, I got THE letter—Uncle Sam Wants You!!!!

"Who, me?!!?"

"Yes, Barry, you!! And, say hello to Vietnam!!"

I had developed a level of cockiness, thinking that I could always get my way. I carried that cockiness with me as I traveled back to

Tennessee to the Selective Service Board to "fight" the draft notice.

The matronly, stern-faced woman I encountered listened patiently as I went through my reasoning for not being drafted. I explained that I was working with a couple of young ladies at Cypress Gardens who both had boyfriends serving in someplace called Vietnam. I went on to explain to the lady that these young ladies' morale was very low and that I could better serve by helping them keep their sprits up.

She listened patiently, then, with a smile, responded, "Young man, I understand your predicament, but you have two choices. Number one, you can report for swearing in and report to the Army Reception Center, or number two, you can always go to jail."

Herman, you were a ferocious warrior, and I often think of your resolve and uplifting attitude when we were preparing to meet such violence. Bullets flying, sounds of combat, images of *young men lying mortally wounded, bodies torn, and screams from the wounded.*

Then it happened—twice. The first time, you saved my life. The second cost you your life.

Our helicopter had been damaged by incoming bullets and exploding rockets. I was lying on the jungle floor with a crushed leg, unable to move and feeling that I was being used for target practice by the enemy. Being wounded in the legs and stomach, a small piece of an exploding grenade sticking in bone between my eyes, my blood was everywhere and you covered me, never receiving a scratch. You stayed with me until you could carry me to the Medevac helicopter.

After I was evacuated back to the world, via Japan, for surgery and rehab, I learned of your second courageous act, which resulted in your supreme sacrifice.

Herman, you loved your Brothers and you fought valiantly, though you did not even know how much courage you had. Your service to our nation and your willingness to shoulder whatever burden placed before you serve as a model for those who came after you.

When I learned you had made the supreme sacrifice, there was a deep crevasse in my heart. Remembering our talks about family, my listening to your "foreign language" about God and your fiancée have echoed in my memories ever since.

After being released from the Army hospital, I was assigned the dreadful duty as a Notification Officer, charged with notifying a soldier's loved ones of their supreme sacrifice in Vietnam – "On behalf of the Secretary of the Army, I regret to inform you that your son/husband has made the supreme sacrifice in Vietnam due to . . ." Needless to say, this duty was personally heartbreaking and I "wrongly" reverted to blaming God for putting me in that spot.

When we returned, many, if not most, Vietnam veterans were labeled as drunks, drugs addicts and "baby killers". It seemed to be the nature of the country at the time. Riots, marches against the war, protesters. Many veterans were even advised to change from army clothing to civilian clothing before traveling home. Again, after my stint in the hospital, and feeling proud of my service, I dressed in my Army Blues and went to a very small church (I was not a member and had never attended there before) thinking maybe I could begin to understand your "foreign language". The young preacher called me aside and asked that I leave because ". . . the House of the Lord does not accept baby killers". Leave I did, accepting that that was further confirmation that God still did not love or accept me. Of course, in retrospect, I was wrong – it wasn't just about me, but the preacher's opposition to anything Vietnam. To the church's credit, I understand that the preacher was asked to leave, or he was fired, without a recommendation.

Today I guard your memory. I remember and cherish you.

Herman, my memories and heart have written long letters to you over the years. You may have saved my physical life, but it took almost twenty more years for my life to be saved by finally understanding, and accepting, that "foreign language" you had been speaking as I stood one morning on a Florida beach.

From 1969 to 1990, I lived deep in survivor guilt, depression, feelings of rejection by the country I loved, isolation, nightmares, and wrecked marriages and relationships. While many returning Vietnam veterans turned to alcohol or drugs to drown their memories, my drug of choice was work and making money. Simply said, the harder I worked, and the more hours I spent in those pursuits, the less time my mind went to the horrors of the jungle, my guilt of leaving my Brothers behind—and, tragically, for my mind to dwell on your supreme sacrifice.

My life took a dramatic turn when I was diagnosed with Non-Hodgkin's Lymphoma. Herman, I know it may sound strange, but my life took off like a rocket ship of good as I stood on that Florida beach and accepted Jesus Christ as my Lord and Savior. There've been plenty of disappointments and setbacks, but my walk with God is strong and indefatigable.

Proverbs 3:23:

Then shall thou walk in thy way safely in the way of thy duty and business, without fear.

I learned that my real sickness, for years, had been, first, not believing that God loved and accepted me and, second, my failure to look for, and catch, the happiness, blessings, and opportunities that God provided upon the horizon of every sunrise. With my cancer diagnosis, I finally learned that the only permanent disabilities or illness lie in not realizing and accepting that God had never rejected me. I had allowed the words and actions of mere men (and women) to shape my outlook and beliefs.

Herman, I feel much better that I've finally put my thoughts to paper. To let you know how your actions to save me from my wounds on the battlefield of Vietnam have given me the opportunity to live the ups and downs of a life in the country we both fought for.

I never had a chance to thank you being in my life. Worse, I never had the chance to say good-bye, my Brother.

I'm going to stop here, but I promise I'll write more and often now that I understand and am fluent myself in that "foreign language" you once spoke.

I love you, my Brother, and we will always be together under God's loving care,

Barry

Points To Ponder

_____

_____

_____

_____

_____

_____

_____

_____

_____

Chapter V

During many months in an army hospital for surgeries and rehabilitation, I made a dramatic decision for an altogether different course for my life. A decision that probably would have been different had I understood what Mike was talking about, many years ago, when he asked me, "Barry, people can see my disability, what's yours?"

Having the time while in the hospital to watch TV, read the daily papers and books, I began to see our American culture in a totally different light. Either I hadn't taken the time before to see what was transpiring in our culture, or I hadn't seen our culture changing from the solid family-values culture of earlier eras to one of success meaning chasing wealth and keeping up with the Joneses.

During my time of maturing from living the fun that I could see as a young man, to seeing the horrors of death in the jungles of Vietnam, our culture was seeming to measure (and, to a large extent, does to this day) someone's life success by . . .

- o Do you have the *right* amount of money?

- o Are you living in the *right* house?

- o Do you have the *right* job title?

- o Are you driving the *right* car?

- o Do you wear the *right* clothes?

- o Are you drinking the *right* beer?

- o Do you take the *right* vacations?

- o And, a whole bunch of other *right* inanities

I bought our culture's definition of what I should have and be hook, line, and sinker.

I committed that I would have those things in my life! Why not? Everyone else seemed to be motivated to have those things. Those who had the "right" things were considered a success, while those who didn't were seemingly relegated to some level of social insignificance.

Me be insignificant? No way!

Because I wasn't in a financial position (on army pay) to begin enjoying our culture's *right* things, I set a goal that by the time of my thirty-ninth birthday, I would be in a position of not having to work for anyone else. I would be in a position to no longer needing to follow someone else's orders, be a slave to a time clock, or wait on a paycheck someone else would give me for doing something I didn't enjoy.

After staying in the Army for three more years, I decided to leave. In short order, I began advancing up the ladder from down-the-street-salesman to the upper echelons of corporate management. True to my objectives, I was in a position to stop working for anyone else by the time of my thirty-ninth birthday.

I had the right money, the right house, the right job title, the right clothes, the right car, the right vacations . . . I had it right—or, so I thought at the time!

I could see it all. I had nothing to be a skeptic about. What I couldn't see . . . well, I just didn't need it.

The reality is, however, my life changed dramatically—my defining moment—and I began to see what Mike had not seen in me so many years ago. But, more on this transition in a moment.

After succeeding in the business world, I discovered that while I had been striving so hard to catch what someone else told me I *should* have, I had been in an unbending state of not seeing. And, as I wrote earlier, being in a perpetual state of not seeing the invisible is a risky and discouraging way to live.

Let's take a brief detour. After all, this message *is* about your future. (I present my past to help you see how you, too, can begin to see God and receive His daily blessings.)

Wherever you are in terms of age, gender, or circumstances, your future is before you. Not having a clear, concise vision of what your future will be can paralyze your whole-life approach to your living experience.

If you cannot shape a clear, concise vision of where you are going, you might not take the first step, or the next one, or the one after that to get to where you'd really like to be. You might never start the journey to live dreams that have been safely tucked away while you think, *"That'll never happen, but it makes me feel good to dream and fantasize about it."* You'll do nothing of substance and go nowhere out of fear that you might be taking the wrong step.

It is the fear of taking the wrong step that can propel you into being someone who sits around and waits for your unplanned tomorrows to accumulate and become a collection of wasted yesterdays. That can lead to a life of wasted dreams.

Not having a vision of your future will lead you to follow someone else's idea for *where* you should go in your future, *what* you should do, or *who* you should be.

Not having a clear, well-defined, and concise vision for your future can cause you to remain confused by events of your past, your current situation, or your fear of the future.

Henry Wadsworth Longfellow once said, "Not in the clamor of the crowded street, not in the shouts and plaudits of the throng, but in ourselves are triumph and defeat."

Doubt about the future was the antithesis of my faith, and my faith in everything around me was pretty well non-existent. Eighteen years ago, my belief and faith in God and faith in my fellow man was shallow, at best.

In retrospect, I know I made mistake after mistake in my earlier years following what others said success was and is. Like a lapdog, I followed what others had pre-ordained for what my life *should* be.

During my early business years, maybe I should have known not to look to others, or to try to compare myself to what others had accomplished or what they owned. Maybe I should not have allowed others to set and define my standards for living a successful life, but I did. And I did it with unbridled passion.

I allowed the shouts and cheers of others, media advertising, my work associates, and my desire for the *right* things calling out to me to define what success and happiness would be in my life.

In perfect alignment with acquiring all the *right* things, I caught the disease of what seems to be the microwave mindset of many in our culture: "I want what I want and when I want it."

Unfortunately, for many, this mantra remains the guiding force for living their lives today. In our culture of excess, giveaways, and programs offered to seemingly make everyone equal, it seems to be easier to wait for, instead of to work for, that faraway future held in dreams and fantasies.

In reflecting on my early years—all the days, months, and years of chasing the "right" things—I realized I was not happy and had caught nothing of real meaning.

After leaving the big, always-on-the-go corporate world, earning the big paychecks, and looking forward to my monthly fix of buying some new thing, I found myself wanting for meaning, searching for my own identity, and longing to catch true happiness.

For three or four years, I wandered aimlessly through life, going through the motions of living, wondering why I wasn't happy, making mistake after mistake and feeling a terrible loneliness.

I had been so busy striving to achieve our culture's "right" standards, that it wasn't until I finally understood that my personal definition of success and happiness should have instead been defined by a relationship with God and a spiritual peace of mind.

It was what Mike had not seen in me so many years earlier.

I simply did not have it, because happiness and peace of mind is a highly personal experience. It must be one we "catch" for, and by, ourselves. It's not the job, the paycheck, the houses, the cars, the clothes, the family, the friends, or any of the other "right" things that lead us to "catching" happiness and peace of mind.

Points To Ponder

_____

_____

_____

_____

_____

_____

_____

_____

_____

Chapter VI

My real-life drama began one chilly morning in 1990. Just before sunrise, I stood on the beach in Florida after having just received the news that would change my life . . . or end it.

"Mr. Rice, your cancer is late Stage III or early Stage IV."

My diagnosis? Non-Hodgkin's lymphoma. A result of my being exposed to the herbicide, Agent Orange, during my service in Vietnam.

Here's the scary part. The doctors then went on to say something like, "Mr. Rice, your cancer is terminal. You may have as little as twelve to eighteen months. We can make you comfortable with drugs, but there's not much more that can be done."

As I stood there on the beach, alone and scared, I kept replaying all the words I'd heard, "Barry, the best that we can advise is for you to go home and enjoy as much life as you can. There really isn't anything that can be done, but don't give up hope for a cure."

Not being able to sleep, I drove out to the beach and walked down to the surf's edge, losing myself in the cool, beautiful, pre-dawn, star-lit morning.

My thoughts were going in every direction and I was questioning everything—including my faded and one-dimensional belief in God.

To that point, I had been a one-dimensional believer in God— believing in Him, but never really accepting that He believed in me. I'm not proud of it, but as with my tendency to the see-touch-feel rule, I had never seen God.

I found myself whining and ranting at the unfairness of it all, sitting firmly on my pity-pot, screaming questions at some invisible force in the pre-dawn sky.

- o "Why me?"

- o "What have I done wrong?"

- o "What did I ever do to You?"

- ○ "What am I supposed to do now—just stand here and fade away?"

When my ranting and wallowing in my self-pity began to subside, my panic and rage did, too.

Probably an hour passed, until I found myself speaking into the wind.

- ○ "God, if you're real, can you see me?"

- ○ "Can you hear me?"

- ○ "God, if you're real, and you believe in and accept me, then what am I supposed to do now?"

I needed an answer. I suppose I was demanding an answer!

In any event, I somehow willed myself to be still and listen, to see if there really was some force in that starlit sky that was listening. The earthly doctors hadn't told me anything I wanted to hear—why not do something completely out of character for me . . . simply shut up and listen.

Feeling as if my feet were sunk into cement, I silently stood there . . . waiting. Waiting for what, I really didn't know.

It wasn't long before the distant horizon began to lighten, and the brightness of the stars began to fade. The top of the sun began peaking above the horizon, beginning its very slow, deliberate climb into the morning sky—clearly and magnificently.

My feelings of self-pity subsided as I began to think how the sun rose every morning, regardless of the circumstances of the world, the weather, who was president, the price of gas, how much money I had in the bank, or because of what anyone else did or said.

But, just as quickly, I slipped back into resisting the beginnings of feeling comfortable, recalling my earlier comfort level of sitting on my pity-pot, blaming others for my situation and fear.

Wanting to remain in the darkness and wishing the sunrise and the new day to simply go away, my thoughts turned to, "I can't do that. I can't make the sun rise; make it go sideways, make it go back down."

The feeling washed over me that if I, or any other person or power I knew, could not make the sun rise, then there must be some power much greater than any mortal who *does* make the sun rise. There had to be some higher power that was making the sun rise every day—no matter the pain, confusion, or daily circumstances everyone faces in their life.

Just suppose, I thought, that there really is a God who creates our days, our nights, our brightness, and our darkness? With those thoughts I found myself asking into the wind . . .

- o "God, if you're there, have you been beside me all along?"

- o "If that's you making the sun rise, did you really need to give me terminal cancer to finally get my attention?"

Were my questions being answered as I became absorbed in the brightening majesty of the sunrise sending its rays shimmering across the waves at me?

It was as if some power was reaching out to me, merely waiting for me to reach out my hand. Feelings of smallness and a sense of humility began to wash over me, and I lifted my hand to reach out.

I looked around. I was alone with the ocean, its timeless tides, wave after wave and mile after mile of empty beach. Was I also alone with God?

Gulls were floating on gusts of wind. Porpoises were dancing just offshore welcoming their new day and celebrating the amazing, perpetual, and enduring sunrise.

The sun's rays slowly began to spread over the beach, glancing off the waves. The sun's beacon pointed directly at me and was beginning to wrap me in its arms of warmth.

The rays bathed me against the coolness of the morning. I felt illuminated in the presence of whatever the power was bringing forth the daily sunrises.

It was as if I felt a hand was on my shoulder, and I began to hear an inaudible voice. It didn't take long to come to the belief that this Power who created the daily sunrise, into infinity, could *only* be God. What other power could bring such brightness and life to each new day? And, do it day after day after day?

It had to be God, the One who had endured all my years of folly and my chasing after, and catching, the "right" things I could see. Even with my previous one-dimensional belief in Him, He displayed with His sunrise, and affirmed for me that morning, that my life would not be over until He chose to stop my sunrises. My life would not be over until He put His "period" at the end of my earthly presence.

God, who my skeptic's mind had, for years, made nearly invisible, was standing before me—disguised as a sunrise.

He was giving me another day to live, another sunrise, and at least one new day to do with as I saw fit. It was His inaudible voice telling me . . .

> *"Barry, you've got this day added to your earthly life, and I'm offering you blessings and opportunities to do with this day as you see fit."*

Some people naturally mature into the depth of meaning and blessings and opportunities of every new day. For many, like me, it took a serious illness, injury, or some personal tragedy to frighten us enough to wake up and start to see the blessings and opportunities God presents every day to live with hope and positive action—one day at a time.

Upon first arriving at the beach that morning, and standing at water's edge, I felt bankrupt of spirit and powerless as a grain of sand upon which I stood to do anything about my situation.

I was alone, discontent, and desperately searching for a way out of the stark terror of my recent medical news.

But, as the sun continued its slow, deliberate climb, my eyes, for once, opened to the acceptance of new hope and so did my heart.

I could see it and I was beginning to feel it. A power much greater than I. Greater than anything I had ever witnessed. I was beginning to *see*, for the first time, the power, the strength, the hope, and the unwavering love and optimism of God!

Across the great divide from where I stood that morning, the horizon glimmered. It appeared calm and inviting.

With the beacon of the sun's rays bouncing off the sea and enveloping me with its warmth, one side of the horizon seemed to appear brighter than the other.

The left side of the horizon appeared much brighter. As I looked out to the brightness, my thoughts went to the scores of people I saw and associated with every day who appeared to be happy, healthy, productive, successful, kind, and giving. They were the people I had ignored for so many years, yet they were the very people who were, and are, enjoying positive, daily living experiences.

They seemed to have purpose, and they had all the *right* things:

- o Financial house was in order

- o Satisfying jobs and careers

- o Strength of family relationships

- o Were always in pursuit of new skills and new knowledge

- o Were taking care of their physical health

- o Were enjoying friends and community

- o Were enjoying peace of mind and a loving relationship with God

It was as if God was directing me to see these people. To see those who are enjoying His bounty, His trusts, living in community with each other.

God was showing me, with His sunrise, people who are seeing and catching His blessings and opportunities, and living their lives, on a day-to-day basis, to their highest potential and beyond!

I began to feel that God was showing me how I could be united with these positive people in some kind of divine kinship. He was showing me how I could also have a daily relationship with Him. To have a relationship with the One who has the power to create the sunrise in the first place, and who is presenting me with the blessings and opportunities to have it all.

God had been presenting me with these blessings and opportunities to "catch" a rich, full life all along—it was me who had been too blinded to see.

But, then along came my skeptic—the defeatist.

I turned my head, looked to my right, to the darker side of the horizon, and was reminded of other people I saw every day. I was reminded of people who were neither happy, healthy, productive, successful, kind, nor giving.

Their lives seemed to be lacking, like mine had been. They were financially, physically, family, jobless, or spiritually hungry.

You've seen them, too. You see people on the darker side of the horizon, every day, ensnared in crime, drugs, financially wanting, without family relationships, homeless, jobless, and seemingly mindless.

These people had reached out to parts of the living experience that I didn't want anymore. Or, perhaps they were simply too lazy and weren't reaching out for the positive blessings and opportunities on the left side of the horizon.

As I continued to stand there, it hit me like a ton of bricks. I had lived my life, to a large degree, on the darker side of the horizon.

Sure, maybe I had been able to *catch* money and the other *right* things that our culture says to have, but I didn't have the opportunities God was displaying on the bright side of the horizon.

My point is, the future is ripe with opportunities and it is up to you and me, individually, to choose the success or failure we desire. It's up to us to choose the side of the horizon that attracts us—and, then to reach out and be responsible for the opportunities we choose.

God never takes away our free will to make choices.

God had done His part that morning, as He does every morning with His sunrise—whether we choose to see it—or not.

He had brought forth that morning's blessing of *seeing* Him, and He seemed to be granting me at least one more day's amnesty from my fears of losing my life to a terrible disease.

With God offering to walk hand-in-hand with me to the positive side of the horizon, my part was to now exercise my free will and take responsibility for the choices I would make for just that day. Because of the realization that my life to that point had been lived on the darker side of the horizon . . .

- o I could choose to be depressed by my cancer doctor's report.

- o I could choose to believe I couldn't move forward because of the economy.

- o I could choose to worry that the forecasted clouds would keep me from seeing the sunrise's positive opportunities on a daily basis.

- o I could choose to complain because of the politics of the day.

- o I could choose to seek pity.

- o I could choose financial ruin.

- o I could choose to distance myself from family and friends.

- o I could choose to ignore my physical body and any treatments to living with cancer.

- o Or, I could choose to put a stop to *seeing* God again.

Or, I could look to the positive opportunities on the left side of the horizon and choose to dream and plan for more of God's blessings and sunrises of opportunity to come.

I could choose to *see* and live a happy, healthy lifestyle.

I could choose to create a vision for just that day and look to future goals and begin to enjoy crafting a whole-life approach to whatever future I had. I could choose to be successful and significant for however many new sunrises I was granted. I could choose to be Moving Forward Out of the Fog. Moving out of the fog that I had lived in for so many years.

Just as that moment of choices, truth, and clarity seemed firmly within my grasp, my skepticism and fear returned with a vengeance—clouding and sabotaging my newfound *seeing* of God.

My skepticism and fears were telling me that there was no way I deserved a rich, full life or any of the positive blessings and opportunities that God was presenting for me to grab. I began to justify myself that I didn't deserve the good stuff, and I hadn't always measured up.

I had not always been a 'good boy.' My past had been littered with over-indulgences, selfishness, and sins, along with my failure to be the well-rounded, loving person I should have been.

My self-worth was taking a beating. I turned around, resigned to the belief that I did not deserve the good things, and began walking away from the water's edge—away from the sunrise and away from God.

With faithless eyes, I hung my head and looked down at the shadow I was creating by my body blocking the sun's rays.

There it was—the big, bad shadow of me. It was the shadow of my past, full of guilt, fault, sin, shame, and broken promises.

Since after my army days, I had forsaken God, family, and friends, all the while looking out for myself and my ability to catch the right things our culture said to have or to be.

I wanted to reach down and wrestle that shadow from my past, wipe him off the face of the earth, bury him in the sand, or scrape him up and throw him away.

But, how could I? How could I change even one thing in my past?

I realized that nothing could be done to change my past. I was powerless to do one single, solitary thing to change anything about who I had been, what I had done, where I had been, or even how I had gotten to that morning.

But this Power, who I had come to believe and accept as God, was presenting me with new blessings and opportunities for a whole-life approach to living for just that day, and He wasn't done yet.

His hand was still on my shoulder as I stared at my shadow, reminding me of His presence and urging me to turn around. He was telling me that I was forgiven, that my past is my past and telling me that even He couldn't change any of my free-will choices of my past.

The free-will thing was popping up again along with my opportunity to make choices for just that day. Do I choose a newfound faith in God? Do I choose to put rugged individualism to work in living for just that day with the blessings I was being offered upon the bright and positive side of the horizon?

OR, do I choose fear and allow my *unplanned* tomorrows to accumulate and be added to my long list of *wasted* yesterdays.

Do I stand with my back to God and let the long, dark shadow of my past tarnish my vision of what that day could be? Do I forgo God's blessings for whatever days lay ahead—whether it be one day, one week, eighteen months, or twenty years?

Do I hang my head, slump my shoulders, and sink into the shadow of my past and wait for my cancer to take my life? Do I choose to drown in my own drama?

Which would it be?

With God's hand on my shoulder, and His reminding me that His Son had died for my sins, I turned around to His glorious sunrise to choose, just for that day, from the blessings and opportunities He was offering upon the left side of the horizon.

Turning back to the sunrise, and walking back to the water's edge, the waves reached my feet and were lapping at my ankles. The farther out to sea I looked, the larger and more formidable the waves had become.

But here's the thing. I saw them as the obstacles and problems I would face in my pathway to accepting and living the blessings and opportunities I would choose. How could I possibly get to the horizon where the good stuff was waiting with those waves of obstacles blocking me?

There were all kinds of waves—little ones at my feet and big, rolling monster waves farther out. They reminded me of the problems and obstacles we create for ourselves, those we allow others to create for us, and those that God might put in our path to strengthen us.

Even so, the waves came between where I was standing and where I wanted to go, just like obstacles that are always in our individual journeys through life. Then I remembered something someone had said to me many years ago . . .

"God may give us a Cadillac, but He won't drive it for us."

Of course, back when I first heard it, I just sloughed it off, thinking, "I don't need anyone to give me anything. I'll *catch* it myself."

I had never been a stranger to obstacles. I had been challenged before by my career choices, skill level, lack of education, experience, and low finances. And, now, I was facing the biggest obstacle of them all—my potential loss of life.

As an aside, we have the choice to either give up when we are confronted by obstacles, or we plan for them, face them head-on, and allow what we learn from them, and our resulting personal growth, to change us for the better.

Moving forward, I again looked at the waves between the horizon of blessings and positive opportunities where I wanted to be and where I was standing. I knew that I could swim my way through them, but the thought of swimming through miles and miles of obstacles seemed futile. There had to be a better, easier, and more creative way.

God coaxed me to the answer.

He showed me how I could build a bridge from where I was standing, supported by the strength of pillars, across the impassible waves of obstacles to the horizon where I wanted to be.

The first pillar of my bridge would be a clear, specific *vision* of what I wanted my future to be—just for that day and with God's continued blessings, many more days to come.

It would not be a vision of "I'd like to have," "Maybe I'll have that someday," "That sure would be nice." The strength of the first pillar told me that my vision would be "I *will* have." My vision of my future would be strong and steadfast. It would be a vision I could continue to build upon, regardless of how much time I had to live—one day, one week, or twelve months.

And, make no mistake! That's the exact amount of time you have right now, and with God's blessings, many happy, fulfilling years to come.

I found, as will you, that this first pillar of having a vision of what the future will be is the most important and most difficult to build as it requires digging deeply into our authentic selves.

Thomas Wolfe, one of the great writers of the twentieth century, said, "So, then, to every man his chance—to every man, regardless of his birth, his shining opportunity—to every man his right to live, to work, to be himself, to become whatever his manhood and his vision can combine to make him."

I would build my first pillar upon my dreams and motivation—made from what makes me come alive, what's important to me, for just that day, and for whatever days I had remaining. These dreams would come from the blessings and opportunities God was displaying upon the horizon.

I would support my vision with realistic goals. I would set goals that are supportive of my vision. Then, I would develop activity plans that would lead to goal achievement.

It became a vision from my heart, just for that day. It became my vision of what my immediate—and long-term life would be. Not a vision formed from the hearts or minds of others who do not know or care about me. My vision of what my future would be, what expressed me, and who I truly was would be my acceptance of walking with God, who was presenting me with tremendous opportunities for just that day.

After beginning to feel comfortable with my vision, supporting goals and activity plans, God showed me that the second pillar of my bridge to the horizon, as I mentally built my bridge, would be *willingness* to carry on.

I must be willing to greet each new day fueled by my renewed faith in God and . . .

- o Faith that even if it was to be my last day, I would be willing to work to achieve the goals that supported my vision of my future.

- o I would be willing to set and put my goals in writing, because the process works.

- o I would be willing to spend whatever time was necessary to develop and write an action-oriented plan to achieve the goals that would fulfill my vision.

- I would be willing to be counted among the 5 percent of people who set goals and reach them 95 percent of the time.

- I would be willing to discipline myself, to work for, to be dedicated to, to educate myself, to give of myself, to share what I can with others and do whatever it is that I must do to realize and live my vision for that day.

- I would be willing to be courageous and unwavering and step out of my comfort zone.

- Most importantly, I would be willing to drive the Cadillac that God was giving me every day to *catch* my vision.

The third pillar for my bridge to living my vision would be *commitment* to stay the course.

- I would not tire. I would not make excuses.

- I would not allow myself, or other's opinions, to sidetrack or derail me.

- o I would stay faithful, focused, and dedicated to my tasks at hand.

- o I would move forward with the feeling in my gut, "I will not be denied."

That early morning was a pivotal point in my life. It was the wake-up call—the "ah-hah!" moment—my ultimate eye-opener.

- o I saw God's blessings and opportunities for the blessings that they were—and the sunrise remains so to this day.

- o I saw God as the only doctor that counts. I saw Him as the only One who could put a "period" to my earthly existence.

- o I saw His sunrise of positive choices of opportunities spread before me upon the horizon.

- o I accepted that the opportunities were there even when murky clouds of my own confusion and the minor inconveniences of living that, at times, make them harder to see.

o I built my bridge that morning to carry me to God's blessings and opportunities, and I have never looked back.

I have continued to express my daily gratitude to God for each new sunrise, and I'm confident that I'll thrive, just for today, living my vision built upon the blessings and opportunities God presents me with each new day.

I will also do my best to live my future, each day, abiding by the significance of a quote from well-known motivational author and speaker, Zig Ziglar . . .

"If I lovingly and generously help enough other people get what they want, I'll get everything I want."

The bottom line is, not only do I continue to cheat my earthly doctor's predictions for the length of my life, but God has blessed me with more of the *right* stuff. He has blessed me with a wonderful life companion, my wife Ann, earning even more money, a wonderful home, the opportunity to travel, my church, new cars, friends, community, and the opportunity to share with others.

God has blessed me with so much more than before when I was so busy forsaking Him in pursuit of the right stuff that society had told me I must have—and who I had to be to consider myself a success in our culture.

All gratitude and faith must go to God, who will continue to have His hand on my shoulder as I walk across my bridge to the horizon of His blessings and opportunities. Every day I envision myself walking or running across my bridge. I can visualize God's blessings and opportunities even while dealing with traffic jams, during thunderstorms, while going through any circumstances that might arise, and over the countless interruptions that attempt to sneak into my busy, daily life.

I have a clear choice. I can allow fears, confusion or minor irritations to rob me of my peace and forward movement to the good stuff, or I can succumb and lose those precious moments of my living experience. You have that choice as well.

Points To Ponder

_____

_____

_____

_____

_____

_____

_____

_____

_____

_____

Chapter VII

Through the years, God has challenged me with other situations to overcome, as well as other physical challenges, that others might choose to call obstacles to living a full, rich life. I label them all as "minor inconveniences" compared to the blessings and opportunities God presents me each day as part of my rich, full life.

Each of my physical challenges initially shook me to the core and maybe appeared insurmountable at the time. But, in the final analysis, none of them have proved to be anything more than a blip during my journey to catching and living my happiness.

Since that morning on the beach, and my acceptance that I could choose and catch my vision—not society's *right* stuff— upon the horizon of God's sunrise of opportunity, each of life's inconveniences has yielded a benefit that was invisible at the onset.

For example, I began having problems, again, with affected lymph nodes and after they were excised at the VA Hospital in Gulfport, Mississippi, I was told that my Non-Hodgkin's

Lymphoma prognosis was once again grim. I was asked if I would accept being a "test subject" for an experimental, new chemotherapy drug that could be administered at the Buffalo, New York VA Hospital, Denver VA Hospital or Nashville VA Hospital. Doctors further told me that known chemotherapy drugs for my type of cancer, or radiation by itself, would no longer keep my cancer in passive state.

My dear reader, I know that snow is beautiful and is an attribute of Mother Nature, but I just don't like being in it. Therefore, I chose Nashville, figuring it would have less of that stuff.

So, the Veteran's Administration sent me to Nashville, Tennessee, for experimental chemotherapy treatment at the VA Hospital, to be administered in conjunction with a Doctor from Vanderbilt University Medical Center. I began taking this new, oral chemotherapy drug five days a week. The other two days a week, I received radiation and continued this regimen for 3 years.

Initially, this transfer was not something I desired, but God proved He was in control and led me to choosing Nashville for my treatment, as He already knew that I would meet my new best friend and now my wife, Ann. Try as I did to convince Ann that she probably ought to be free to pursue her life, free of standing by me for those three years of cancer treatments, God led Ann to stand by my side – and, I'm the luckiest man in the world that I shut up and listened. Plus, I discovered my church home and an ever-expanding circle of supportive friends and community activities to be actively involved in. God also led me to opportunities to give back through our church and community activities.

Blessings continued to flow from my newfound relationship with God. After no longer having my corporate work to mask my memories of combat, death, and destruction in Vietnam, I began experiencing PTS (Post Traumatic Stress) —nightmares, flashbacks, survivor's guilt, and isolation tendencies to shroud my memories. With Ann's understanding and learning all she could about PTS and encouraging me to be involved with other veterans by giving back, God led me to leadership positions with Vietnam Veterans of America.

With everything that had been swirling around me, my financial life had taken a severe downturn. Accepting that I was broke, not poor, God guided me to people who supported my abilities and desires to work with others. My financial life recovered and thrived, and continues to this day to increase like never before.

In 1999, I underwent quadruple-bypass heart surgery, due to, once again, my exposure to Agent Orange in Vietnam. As a result, God led me to a new appreciation for physical fitness and living a healthy lifestyle.

I then underwent left hip and left knee replacement as final repairs of old wounds and injuries from Vietnam. God's blessings of these surgeries relieved me of thirty years of ongoing pain and an inability to get the most out of my overall physical fitness conditioning. Interestingly, in order to undergo those surgeries, it was necessary that I be removed from the five-day-a-week chemotherapy treatments. I was taken off that nasty stuff, and my doctors have not seen it necessary to start it again.

Although I have been told that I will need to continue a form of radiation for the rest of my life, God has blessed me, working through my earthly doctors, with being able to secure a portable radiation unit for my home. Being able to take the treatments just before bedtime, three times a week, allows the side effects to be gone by morning, enabling me to continue enjoying my vision—my "right" to life. Prostate cancer was caught early and heightens my gratitude for God's blessings and opportunities.

Let's return to your sunrise of opportunities.

Recall, again, the sun rising into the morning sky that you watched that morning and visualize how the opportunities for anything you want in your future were, and are, waiting for you upon the horizon of God's sunrise of blessings and opportunities.

Using your free will, choose from the many opportunities that are the right fit for you today and form a vision of what your future will be . . .

- Experiencing happiness like never before

- Having peace of mind about the direction of your future

- Having renewed enthusiasm for your future

- Enjoying a major boost in your self-confidence and self-esteem

- Putting financial worries behind you

- And, most importantly, a spiritually based peace of mind

The next question to ask yourself: "Can I let go of my past mistakes, sins, or overindulgences and remember that they are nothing more than images in my mind from the shadow of my past?"

Now, accept that God has already relieved you of those burdens from your past through His blessings of forgiveness?

Once you have turned back to face your sunrise, it's time to identify the obstacles that might stand in your way of moving out to your horizon.

Define any potential obstacles, in advance, as clearly and honestly as you are able . . . and remember that God will never present you with more that you can handle. You'll discover that most of the obstacles that you think are there will also become minor inconveniences when compared with the positive blessings and opportunities God has waiting for you.

The timing is right, right now, to begin building your bridge to the positive opportunities and future waiting for you upon the horizon of your many sunrises to come.

With each new sunrise comes a new day. Twenty-four hours packed with promise and offered as a blessing by God who gives us the sunrise in the first place.

It's time to form a clear vision of what your future will be—a vision that will not grow dark with fear, shame, or sadness. It will be a vision supported by effective goals and fulfilled by realistic planning of the activities required to achieve your goals.

Walt Disney died in 1966 shortly before EPCOT was completed. At his passing, someone commented that what a shame it was that he never lived to see this idea realized.

But he *did* see it—that's why it's there. Nothing becomes real until it is first held as a vision.

Your second pillar is your willingness to move forward and to do the work necessary to drive your Cadillac to living your vision. Are you willing to . . .

- ○ Start each morning with gratitude for God's new sunrise and the blessings and opportunities presented upon the horizon?

- ○ Let go of your past mistakes, sins and over-indulgences?

- ○ Forsake what others may be telling you that you should have or who you should be?

- ○ Clearly define what your future WILL be (NOT "I'd sure like to have," "Someday," "That'd be nice," etc.)?

- ○ Spend whatever time is necessary to set effective goals that support your vision, not goals that conflict with your vision as you see it?

- ○ Take the necessary action-steps to achieve your goals?

- ○ Take a deep breath at the end of each day just to say, "Thank you God for all of the blessings You are bringing to my life?"

The final pillar—and this is vitally important—is your burning-in-the-belly desire to drive the Cadillac that God is presenting to you to travel to your dreams. It's your unyielding commitment.

It is the knowledge that you now have all the information about your visions; that you have mapped out your path and that you will NOT be denied.

Living in concert with God, who gives us The Power and Blessings of a Sunrise, reminds me of the story of the mother whose young son loved to play the piano.

Wanting to encourage his progress, she looked forward to taking him to a concert given by the famous Polish pianist, Paderewski. When the evening arrived, they found their seats near the front of the concert hall and eyed the impressive stage. The mother engaged herself in conversation with a friend seated to her left and became oblivious to what was going on around her, including what her son was doing.

At eight o'clock, when the lights in the auditorium dimmed and the spotlights came on, the little boy was sitting on the bench of the great Steinway and innocently plucking out "Twinkle, Twinkle Little Star."

The mother gasped in horror, but before she could retrieve her son, the master pianist appeared on stage, quickly moving to the keyboard. He hovered over the boy whispering, "Don't quit. Keep playing." Paderewski then reached down with his left hand and began filling in the bass part. Soon his right arm reached around the other side of the boy and improvised a delightful duet.

Together, the master and the boy made great music.

This same scenario applies to your future. You're standing on the beach. God has appeared before you, disguised as a sunrise, as the opportunities you have chosen for your future are revealed. But you'll also see something else.

As you look to God, you will see the sun's rays reflecting and bouncing across the waves. Those are none other than the mighty arms of God as He is whispering to you, "Don't quit, keep playing."

Through His daily sunrise, even on days of confusion, murkiness about your future, the pressure of daily circumstances, and your minor inconveniences, God will always extend His arms to you and urge you to move forward across your bridge.

And, so it is when you invite God to put His arms around you as He presents you with The Power and Blessings of a Sunrise.

When we accept God's love and we trust Him with our hearts, our lives, and our very beings, even on the cloudiest of days, our eyes will open to the blessings, opportunities, and happiness that await us as we build and walk across our bridges to catch our vision.

In closing, let me tell you the famous Vince Lombardi story. His returning Super Bowl champion Green Bay Packers arrived at training camp to begin preparations to achieve their goal of repeating as champions of the National Football League. As they walked onto the field to begin their warm-ups and practice, his first words to the team were "Gentlemen, THIS is football."

Mr. Lombardi was taking them back to the basics that had gotten them to the championship in the first place. The basics of rugged individualism, collectively working together, and sharing would return them to the championship.

Going back to the basics with your rugged individualism will always work in all areas of your endeavors as well—especially in catching the opportunities being presented to you daily by God with The Power and Blessings of a Sunrise.

I invite you to build your bridge upon the strength of the pillars of your *Vision, Willingness,* and *Commitment* by putting The Power and Blessings of a Sunrise to work for your future.

The power who gives us the sunrise of daily blessings and opportunities—God—is awaiting your decision. Are you going to stand up and receive His blessings for a rich, full future of living your vision? Are you going to drive, with rugged individualism, the Cadillac that is being so graciously given you by God in order to *catch* your happiness?

Thank you and my best wishes to you for a lifetime of bountiful opportunities and blessing-filled sunrises.

Points To Ponder

_____

_____

_____

_____

_____

_____

_____

_____

_____

Made in the USA
Columbia, SC
18 September 2019